WORKING FIREWOOD FOR THE NIGHT

WORKING FIREWOOD
FOR THE NIGHT

Poems by Lloyd Van Brunt

The Smith **Brooklyn**

Published by The Smith, 69 Joralemon Street, Brooklyn, New York 11201
Typography by Pineland Press, Waldoboro, Maine 04572
Printed at Capitol City Press, Montpelier, Vermont

Library of Congress Cataloging in Publication Data:

Van Brunt, Lloyd, 1936 —
Poetry
ISBN: 0-912292-88-1 (paperback)
        0-912292-89-X (cloth)
                    89-92768 CIP
First Edition

Artwork © 1990 by Jim Kay
Back cover photo © 1988 by Kathy Morris

Acknowledgments

Grateful acknowledgment is made to the following journals for permission to reprint poems that originally appeared in their pages: *The American Poetry Review; The American Writer; Another Chicago Magazine; The Antietam Review; Blueline; Confrontation; Fell Swoop; The Georgia Review; The Greenfield Review; Long Pond Review; New Letters; Poet Lore; Poetry Australia; Poetry Now; Pulpsmith; South Dakota Review; Southern Poetry Review; Tulsa Poetry Alliance; The Washingtonian; West Branch; Wind; Witness;* and *Wyoming.*

"Meditation on Matthew Arnold" and "Untitled" were first published in *The American Poetry Review.* Copyright © 1990 by World Poetry, Inc.

"The Girl Who Learned to Pose for Photographers" and "Speech After Long Silence" were reprinted in the anthology, *Only Morning in Her Shoes.*

"Smallmouths" was reprinted in the anthology, *The Cooke Book: A Seasoning of Poets.*

"A Seabird Poem for Children" and "True North: A Celebration of American Womanhood" were reprinted in the *Anthology of Magazine Verse & Yearbook of American Poetry.*

Also by Lloyd Van Brunt

Uncertainties
The Smith, 1968

Indian Territory and Other Poems
The Smith, 1974

Feral: Crow-Breath and Caw
The Conspiracy Press, 1976

For Luck: Poems 1962-1977
Carnegie-Mellon University Press, 1977

And the Man Who Was Traveling Never Got Home
Carnegie-Mellon University Press, 1980

CONTENTS

for Julie

and in memory of Laura M. Conan
25 December 1933
23 November 1989

Magic Turns:

The Poetry of Lloyd Van Brunt

I am deeply moved by Van Brunt's poetry. There is a delicacy, a kind of gnawing knowledge, that is overwhelming. One often speaks of the pity and the sadness at the heart of things, of all living things, and that is the wave length that Van Brunt is on, though I perhaps make that sound too much like a strategy — it is rather an essential part of his make-up. It is his character.

I find his lucidity appealing, his tenderness, his sense of loss. His is the poetry of ruin, a poetry that is written after the events have taken place, so to speak, and all that is left is the pity, as Wilfred Owen says. It is perhaps because of his native American heritage that he writes like this, it is perhaps because he spent his youth in an orphanage, stripped of family, brutally stripped of love, in the hands of the matrons he writes about. Yet there are other elements in his poetry or we would just have sad elegies. There is sometimes a certain terror, almost an uncontrolled terror, that moves the reader deeply; there is moral outrage, a sense of justice, anger; and there is wisdom and rueful cunning that comes from long years of experience.

I try to place these poems in the history of recent literature and I find it difficult. I believe there is an original voice. What characterizes the style is music, an attempt to create loveliness, and it is that attempt, and an overwhelming attention to details, to things in the world, to an acceptance of those things and almost a faith in them, that makes his poetry finally a poetry of acceptance and not a poetry of rejection. He comes out of a realistic tradition, he is a remarkable observer, and his metaphors are always based on things in the real world, on things he has seen and realized. I suppose Hart Crane is the poet he is closest to, Hart Crane and perhaps a little William Carlos Williams. Certainly from a point of view of the music, the attention to the world, and the love of lyric, he is a descendant of Crane.

These are mature poems, and exceptionally well crafted. Van Brunt has achieved a mastery, and he writes, it seems, with ease. In a poem like "The Stars Like Minstrels Sing to Blake," he shows this mastery. There is realistic detail, legend, philosophy, and mysticism combined — all in a very personal voice. There are magic turns, elegance, and transcendence, but we are always there with a group of helpless starlings strung out along a wire. Nor do we ever leave his sense of pity and his identity with the helpless. In "Wanda Pickles," there is a voice of experience, a mature — and forgiving — voice coming to terms with childhood malaise and adolescent agony. It is a marvelous poem. And in "Revenants," there is bitter confession and self realization, an overwhelmingly honest understanding of the sources of behavior.

This is a strong collection of poems, a moving book.

Gerald Stern

"How many ancient myths begin with the rescue of an abandoned child!"

— *Milan Kundera*
The Unbearable Lightness of Being

The Stars Like Minstrels Sing to Blake

A wire strung with starlings, all
fluffed and bobbed in a stormy wind
black as their shako tails.
They seem to be squeezing that electric wire.
They seem to be playing it with their feet,
the stops pitched higher than human hearing,
like some kind of music of the hemispheres —
like 24 hands at the same piano.
When they leave together
the way a school of bait-fish jump
from shallows when a shadow
veers into view
the wire that hums volts to this studio
swings like a jump-rope — about to explode
and snap through the window. If you were holding me now
a current of fear might light up your bones like mine.

My grandmother said never reach to help
man, woman, or child that's been struck by
         lightning. Leave them there
on the ground, by a tree, or a tractor. The current remains
live long after the scorched heart
stills in the blazed body
and if you even touch them
you'll light up once and turn dark forever.

Though the stars like minstrels sing to Blake
I don't woo death any more than those birds
that ignorant of science rest
clef feet on a singing wire.
But it's necessary to touch death sometimes.

It's necessary to reach out for bodies
struck by lightning
slumped on city streets these days
superstitious bodies
lying there all exposed
blazed with the mark of Cain —
bundles that might explode
and light you up like a Christmas tree.

Meditation on Matthew Arnold

In the sea the snot
of gangly jellyfish
caught in the surf's singsong
linger at the breasts of children,
tendrils wrestling brine,
as though the eddies there,
the small mouths forming bubbles
reeked of home waters,
bottomless lagoons.

That old knot the heart
frays fitfully
as a breeze continues
lifting lank hair
back from mica-eyes,
and fingers loose their grip
on the chaffy sand.

What is happiness then
that we lie here together,
lumpen flesh glossed
by celestial royalty.
Shall I call you my celebrity?
Shall I say that we make love
eyes opening on one another,
or pan to private images
of TV and movie stars
with the gasping gaze of saints.
Into what extended realms
these ikons of the ideal
flash their keyboard teeth

that we lonely and enchanted
children in a forest
lean to their bewitched
wolf's breath and yellowish eye —
that we mimic in our clownish
zeal their delight
in appearing adorable and bright.

O, love, let us be true ...
to a modest land of dreams,
the body's own topography,
let us never slur a lyric
in our hoarse rendition
of the oldest ballad known to love.

O orbed and glowing princess,
great earth-mother of the stick-figure cave
my distrait and furtive female spirit —
to whom I first devoted
awkward, husky, ardent,
wordless, teen-age verse —
I kiss your painted toenail
the color of *kouroi* lips
one last virginal time,
and banish you to heaven,
to the heights of Helios,
and all your sunspot atoms
to the asbestos stars.

I make a covenant
on this fouled blue planet
with the true twin heart beside me —
whose footfalls echo mine
through a howling bestiary
of the heart's secret self —

not to be abstract,
as art is from life,
too cold with ideals
that never stink or bleed,
or flush with the tension
of glandular obsession —
I walk my ashen lips
along a rib's mountain road,
and scent a rose-temple,
the home where I was born
to make the old lewd devotions
to the sacral flesh.

On the Serengeti

The first rule is survive, you said.
I thought about nature and extravagance —
how thousands of unsteady gazelle
calves go down before scavengers
on the Serengeti — wild dog, hyena,
lion, cheetah bellies raw
with cardinal flesh
that dried and shivered in the sun.
Who knows how large this *corps de ballet*
that moves as a light wind
      on the wide plain.

If injustice then is the order of things,
if all those grand abstract ideas —
fairness, concern for others, duty —
we recited formulas for the meaning of
as rote-happy schoolchildren
go down before the fist and the firing squad —
if nature's bullying bulges the necks
of Marines as well as lions,
why not push our noses in the guts of things,
why not hop the black dance and shriek?

What then if sex is just survival
and loves gives it a kind of dignity
we think we must believe or swoon?
Young gazelles pronk and flash
around one another like butterflies
in sideways exuberance — lion nostrils
flicked with a tail. These may die
but no upheaval of indignity
can sour the sweetest disposition
for having the sheer guts
        to be alive.

I Fall in Love with Nancy Drew

I ruined my eyes reading Nancy Drew,
girl detective. In the gloom,
as twilight fingered the higher branches
of blackjack oak on distant ridges
and acorns dropped from the octogenarian
proper oak in which I propped
book and gullible disposition,
I broke with Nancy out of twisted
side roads dark with trap-door houses
in a yellow roadster that skimmed the
          moon-breathed sea.

I was a student of the human condition
that loneliness accompanies.
Shamed from my mother's tuberculosis,
exiled with those compatriots
whose sleep was shrill, who peed the bed,
I took refuge in the orphanage asylum:
a memorial library some thoughtful widow
stocked with Nancy, Tom and the Twins —
rank on rank of uniform bindings
ascending in order to the cold corners.

I cut the pages of one book a week
        for umpteen years — two in the summer —
with a special sky-blue-handled knife
beneath his picture. The dear departed —
        benign yet stern, a natural "nuncle" —
the dear departed oilman's smile
and firm brown eyes grew irresolute
only in the last low light of winter
(the lamps and fireplace, pristine) —
when even in the rigid precincts of death
he might have longed for the halo
        of one more good cigar.

The Girl Who Learned to Pose for Photographers

My mother's mother was a half-Choctaw Indian
who looked more natural in bare feet
than in those clump-clump tall black shoes
she hid in layered skirts.

Once we saw her, down by the creek,
humming and smiling, skirts up to her knees,
feet spraying the shallows
like schools of minnows.

Our grandmother's homemade quilts felt cold,
lumpy and heavy as our worst moments.
She stitched in scraps what her life had been —
16 children, 4 stillborn —

yet still had a smile, her store-bought teeth
parted for any camera:
She told us how she learned as a girl
to pose for frontier photographers.

We played this game, Grandma as a girl.
My sister giggled when I dictated
"You have to get down on your back," I said,
"and spread your legs, and knock your knees."

I tightened my ass and peeked at my sister's
dirty white underpants. I directed
her on the ground, spindly legs shaking,
with me on top, and then she heaved me

off, "They don't either do *that*," she screamed,
"You don't play fair, you're a *bum*,
you're a dirty old bum." She smoothed her dress
above her knees, and skipped away.

Grandma, if she heard us, might have whispered
love, too, skips away — beware, little children,
the shortest step I ever took
was ... romance to drudgery.

She snipped her last baby's cord at 30,
toothless and deaf, then slept on a pallet,
thighs clamped to male entreaties —
and became the old woman my grandfather called her.

Her real possessions were the photographs
taken of her as a girl
in front of a hogan in Alabama.
The photographer had taught her how to pose
        in the natural light of children's eyes.

The drum she heard in the underbrush
that speckled noon, the dry heat cracking
cicada burrs, the shallows purling
across arthritic ankles, sinking

in fine sand, beat at her skin,
and to it she shuffled, stomped and sloshed
back to childhood in her Muskogean.
My sister giggled to see such ritual.

....

When my grandmother's twisted, fevered hands
and small brown face
exulted again —
as in those noontime fiery shallows —

her swollen feet kicked the hospital-folded
sheets till they broke. She rose, free
one last time from the alien ground —
her cries pure Choctaw smoke
     in the antiseptic light.

Bible, Torah, Koran

Why is it I feel more at home among Jews —
A red-neck goy with these Orientals?
Is it because matrons whipped me in the shower
(for things I didn't do)
With willow switches, and later garden hoses
Were turned on kids whose imaginations turned
On bathrooms ornate as movie stars',
And private as a mausoleum: "Here, you little bastards,
Here's more water!". Lying in a soaking mess all night,
We learned to dream Puritanical.

My sister's convinced that she, too, is Jewish —
That great-grandfather was never a Chief
But an *Ashkenazi* adopted by the tribe
After buffalo hunters turned against the black-
Frocked little man who ate apart
With a cornpone *pogrom* of their own:
His strange possessions scattered over the plains,
His pale wrists mottled by rawhide thongs.

Of course there *was* this affair with a Rabbi
Who must have filled her heart with holy light
At about the time she became convinced
We were changeling Jews — our mother's nose
Not Sitting Bull's but Martin Buber's.

What of it, I say — just as Nina exclaimed
Last Sunday at a *shivah* out on Long Island
As our host was explaining the history of *kosher*
And she shook her shoulders, "I know that".

I know that too, I know the history of suffering
And the diaspora of families
Out on the plains where the whippoorwills cry
Whip-whip-poorwill, and the whole horizon
Falls on the shoulders of the dirty boy
Down by the fence of the orphanage:
"I won't go in [I'm bad if abandoned],
Bad, bad," he overheard himself,
"Dirty and bad, bad and dirty" —
Like wind breaking from his mouth.

I wrote that history in New York
With the help of an older Jewish woman
Who taught me sex was not dirty but a gift —
And the one true solace of human nature
Was what a man and woman sweated for,
Praying together — and in that hosannah
The feral body sang its own salvation.

Smallmouths

All I see are tails
waving through the water,
and circles that startled frogs
began in their descents.
The circles, according to poets,
widen into forever.
I could never imagine that.
I think rather of you —
the way your eyes seem circles
that change into skies —
the way chestnut hair
loosens on your shoulders.
I think of this by a lake
darkened with low clouds.
Lulled on a rock,
I swallow the horizon
with the motion fish breathe —
until their drifting tails
seem to wave goodbye
as the slender smallmouth bass
shoal in deeper water.

Waking and Sleeping

crickets in this weather
might as well be landscape
the way whole hills of them

ring through the night
they are like the surf
of traffic in the distance

only when you listen
only when left out
of your own conversations

does the irregular tide
of the world outside your body
send wave splashing wave

I doze while your soft moans
and rustling of arms
say the same thing

The Contact Negative

On the original
I carefully cut myself,
snag-toothed,
out of the picture.

I remained a silhouette,
following your curves —
the perfect complement
to all of you I knew.

I had you blown up
from one dim Polaroid,
then wrenched apart the print:
I prefer you in reverse,

curling, turning brown.
Bored eyes bright,
you are all goosebumps now
who were insouciant.

I am not listening
to modern chamber music
at some unending party
as we were doing then,

but see in solitude
the figures of a fugue,
as in a silent movie,
run on and on and on:

what remains of love
after 15 years:
the silent, slightest drop
of music in the blood.

The Rain Has Walked Away on Stilts

                    A knock
On the door at dawn will be mine.
Beggars will whine and show you their gums.
You will hold up your hands to the light as you wake —
Half-believing the corpse you held was mine.

We sensed our lives were empty rooms —
That when the other was away
Our eyes were what we had to say,
And they were skies without a moon.

Now shivering in the morning chill
You remember the garden and the rain,
And press your nose, as you did as a child,
Against the beaded windowpane.

The rain has walked away on stilts,
And left a silence dripping still;
And a slightly musty odor
Rises from the windowsill.

We should have packed away our days.
They should lie folded neatly in stacks
In the clean closet of our lives.
Instead we chose to gaze through trees —

Pinwheels, windbells, gold and green
Through limbs the semaphores of leaves
Waved like butterflies —
And opened wings of eyes.

First Draft

I chipped away your immaculate smile
with a hammer so blunt and misshapen
it was like my own physiognomy
inside where the ordinary life
divides from the one imagined —
inside where the spirit phrenologist
measure the creases, the wrinkles, the lines rising up
bitter at the mouth's U-turns
year by invisible year.
This is where what we look like collects —
dirt in the corners, bags weighing the eyes.

This the anonymous face in the car
on sleepless nights that looks out over water
where the roarings meet —
where everything rushes together and apart,
the white spume rising like anger and desire,
when we know that body clumsy in the surf —
its rag-doll gesticulations
relentless as gravity
and our unconscious minds.
This is when lives sound like the sea,
moaning for the warmth of hand that will give them
            back their innocent selves.

I have been muttering all night long
in one of those wishful-thinking dreams
so quick with life, so *cinéma-vérité*
it's like a first novel that begs for revision.
I am deleting the bad, unfaithful parts.
I am revising those years in the Maryland suburb

where love, by repetition, exhausted itself —
leaving bodies
        but no one inside.
I have a new beginning: outraged children,
furious as your red hair,
rush back to life from a false condition —

as if one of them hadn't feigned death to the pale,
and the other believed her doll-like complexion.
Now they rise flushed-faced and nimbly follow
that alchemic monk with silent gesture
(they are Adam and Eve and He is God the Father
and death is not the consequence of pleasure).
        I am de-constructing the less-dramatic chapters:
no Monday-mornings of robot-routine,
no fretting in lines, no traveling intervals,
none of the gritty cinder blocks of time
        that skin the knuckles of our daily lives.

My novel is like one of your photographs,
or a skull-landscape by O'Keeffe.
We see what we see by dramatic contrasts —
the simple eye seduced again
into enlarging the hidden, small
detachments of a bone or shadowed cheek —
the quick recognition
of the human condition —
and real life, as on a film,
is merely the setting, crowds of extras
like background dots going out of focus,
        standing in fuzzy tedium.

Meditation on Matthew Arnold – II

Jellyfish
shipwrecked down the night surf
blink on and off like theatre lights.
They pass from one to another
the sun's first amethyst blaze.
Streaked with veined curlicues
they look, close up, like what's leftover
from the guts of the sea itself.
They dry like stones, dull.

The gulls, this morning, close as gnats,
flap over gouging, slapping fish
whose attention to a shark-torn pilot whale
approaches frenzy.
The whale's skewed U-turn mouth
seems fixed in a kind of benevolent smile —
as though the cat-eyed bluefish swarms
and their winged squawking cousins
were not dismembering a corporeal body
but the ghost of love, from an ancient world —
the ghost of light that last night lay
Venus's pencil path
on a coal-tar-blackened sea.

Love here's a thin wire of excitement,
tingling the belly, it ends in saliva,
and jerks on instinct. Bloody scraps,
sluiced in the emerald-turning tide,
rush back and forth, like flesh in search of bones.
The sea this morning reminds us of —
not love, not moonlight, not romance —

but the skin peeled back to the naked works
of nature's gut —
a great shark's belly sliced wide open
to reveal sleeping fetuses in a row —
sloshing them and half-digested bodies,
buckled tin cans and its own gray entrails
out to air on a salty dock.
I see Geraldo Rivera out to film
this "first time ever" for TV:
SHARK WHO SWALLOWED CRIPPLE CAUGHT!
He holds up two dismembered limbs.
Of course we watch the show, transfixed
from the first close-up, the beast's dangling heart,
the way we viewed our first porno movie
and saw what we looked like in the dark —
when all our granular private parts
that were a neutral boy's or girl's
swelled to the public's property —
we marked then the apparition of the future
as communal, contrived, and engineered —
and that the supreme poet of the twentieth century,
the prophet of technology and the artist's doom,
had been the psychological-advertising man
who 30 years ago as a guest
in an idealistic English class
on World Literature's fatally great
had laughed at Ibsen, Eliot, and Yeats:
"In short, the question today is this:
WHAT KIND OF SHIT SHALL THESE PIGS EAT!"

The sea this morning reminds us of
how petty individual death-shrieks sound
in nature's species-symphony —
and the chords in the surf's old bloody throat
roar in our ears.

A Seabird Poem for Children

Gulls and terns so thick
you could stroke their pigeon necks
with a long feather-duster
if you climbed the cliff ladders,
thermal to the clouds —
if you milled out over meridians
to check bluefish positions
with eyes on a swivel,
and complained in a voice like water
from a well
drawn by a rusty pulley —
if you dozed on roller coasters
and bobbed beyond the surf,
and woke to amber sunlight
or a rainy dawn —
if your temperature was 120
and you ate twice what you weighed
every day to fuel
the jet engines of your wings —
if sometimes arguments
with others of your kind
sounded alien,
so stellar and strange
human eyes held you
as if in recognition
of an ancient conversation —
you might know how a seabird
draws light through its body
from half-mile-high clouds
or what it's like to be lost sight of

on a stormy morning
far out to sea.

The Man Who Ran from His Own Shadow

the beach this morning
scrubbed like the bottom
of a copper pot
sun so new
parallelogram rays
walk the water like stilts
everything landward
moves from the ghost of its night self
sweet simultaneity!
that jump in the gut
like starting an old car
gulls swoon
to John Keats' poem
stalks of grass
bend back like shocks of hair
a trail of footprints
tipped with foam
ankles scythe
sawgrass from sand
and eyes blot
condo-erections
down to the level of their foundations
the sea's moiré
re-claims the horizon
a shining path's
witch-doctor-saint
blesses the foam
& burgundy surf
white man the marginal
& naked cubist
unfurls condo flags

west to the Pacific
the one-tense present
shucked like a snake's skin
look at that man
he's in a film
that's speeded up
& even when pregnant with gravity
his stumble-bum shadow
will never catch up.

Rutting Season Behavior

I'll bet he would have been ten yards
ahead of that bull a sign
nailed to the cottonwood
over in the next pasture
warns can do the 100-yard dash
in 10 seconds flat
(CAN YOU?
WALK AT YOUR OWN RISK!).

Or halt if you clashed together
a pair of antelope antlers
the color of local weather
seized in the shadow
of that slab-sided hill.

The buck nosed the wind
for a moment. The yellow stars
in his eyes flared to nova.
Ripe with momentum
he headed toward the antlers
my hands froze to my head.

A stopwatch heart
ticked unbelievably
for almost eighty yards —
the gaudy 12-point rack
backlit by the setting sun.

**POET GORED TO DEATH
BY MAD MALE DEER
IN THE WILDS OF WYOMING!**

Game warden explains:
"A 240-pound deer
at 30 miles an hour ..."
"Rutting season behavior,"
state biologist says.

He seemed to swerve when the shadow
of that rack reached my knees —
hurtled by so close
he left behind the scent
of rank and urine heat.

His last quarter mile
along the length of a ridge
could not be clocked.

Dirge for the Pileated Woodpecker

1.
The beech projects light,
and sound is provided by
the bird with the comical name —
whose cry seems always strangled
three notes into an aria —
whose drumming threatens the roots
of the dead tree it calls the living
and crawling creatures from —
whose yodeling accompanied Tarzan
(Johnny Weissmuller then)
with authentic African howls
as Muzak to wow Jane.
O, bird, your home should be a jungle,
a habitat
spectacular and contradictory
to match your nature and attire.

2.
Worm-eater and bug-devourer,
the choir-boy voice you take
deeper into the woods
reminds me of my own
when it was breaking up.
I was only twelve
and sang, like Jeannette MacDonald,
the Indian Love Call trill,
then I was guttural,
I was only twelve,
awkward as a rail,
solitary as a thrush,
then without a voice.

"Cat got your tongue?"
Grandmother Perkins
asked me every visiting day.
I knew what it meant to have a funny name —
half-frog, half-prince, half hazy nothing —
and, as my grandmother always told me,
"all peckerwood."

Fairy Tale Apocrypha

Narcissus first dammed water
to use as an enlarger.
Plopped in the pool by self-extravagance
his profile turned frog-blunt
and he was obliged
to grunt to the gods for a bride-of-the-morning.
A sour joke to all Olympus
the troll-prince's tongue-tied laments
chided Gaia, and she allowed
the first replication of frog DNA.
Poseidon seemed bored, not amused
by these mudpie additions
to the blurry world. Narcissus worked
the conveyor belt of himself nights
and snuggled to the Mississippi bosoms
of his squat daughters by the light.

He croaked to the hordes pliéd around
his dying bed, frog love's not noble
but a throat swells to a fine erotic bubble,
and since you could not see yourself
in the well-bottom eyes of your beloved
just struggle closer to the wet-leather
seat of her bottom. Tadpoles not only
add one's genes to the ancestral
pool but are also good to eat.

Leftovers

We honor then small sonorous bodies,
flies, mosquitoes, for their persistence
into November, their allegiance to sticky
surfaces — night's ululations
and alcoholic gesticulations
paralyzed in another dimension:
the stove's white enamel strewn with grounds;
the lacy edges of midnight eggs
curled back into fetuses,
burnt in a sooty skillet.

Signs so blighted, stale, adhesive
they stick in the mind — residuals
from spittle-lies and braggadocio —
O the brute spirit's grope towards love!
Only flies could attach themselves to
the heart's sore decrepitude.
Only the last of this year's mosquitoes,
stellar and ethereal,
would sing on such an early morning
praises to the way blood rises and falls.

True North: A Celebration of American Womanhood

And O, the hay of her hair, the smell,
The sweet American girl self —
The yeast of prairies rising to her cheeks,
The hops in her bones content. I have brushed her

With a beard and without,
I have sung the little birds in her throat asleep,
And dreamed in eastern European cities
Of heat, like peach fuzz, on her limbs. It isn't

That she has more charms than European
Ladies who never shave their legs,
Or bathe no more than twice
A week in the summer. No, it's the American

Loaminess of her — the pure salt wit,
The waves in her eyes when your hand's on her knee,
And how she tosses through the night
To bring you home. O true, *True North!*

On Looking at a Raphael

I'll take those angels there, the ones
toward the back of paradise —
cherubs, seraphim, with fat
cheeks and butts and ruddy complexions.
They must be attached to a part of heaven
where fucking, when permitted, lasts
at least a century —
where lovers short of ideals learn
ideally how to serve
with patience and loyalty and lust
that redheaded huntress-seraph
with eyes the hue of April willows
and a brace of rosy breasts —
a heaven where everything lies blessed
by love, and Jesus' distracted eye.

Sirius

Standing in this field
I hear a different winter
keening through the snow.
The excavated light
caves in the western sky.
I lean against the bark
of a hanging bough,
until I am silent
as the frozen drifts,
until I am dark
as simply what there is.

I play a deeper bass,
more sonorous than wind
tugging at the roots
of icy spruce and fir.
If I could be heard
I should select The Dog
to sing the chorus to —
not for what it is,
cold, decaying light —
but for what it seems ...
a huge, feral wolf

howling through the spaces
a body's florid heat.

Notes Toward a Poem About the National Zoo

1. Prologue — The Wolves

She is all pink, she is all roses,
and her father cradles her
higher so the wolves may see her
and she them; and the big one does
so clearly that his gray-brown body
seems to flow down the man-made slope
as water from a broken dam —
to lap against the fence till his belly
surges up the crest of his almond-
yellow eyes whose light has quickened
the great cerulean blue of hers,
and the brown ones of her father.

O, Father, let me sit beside her,
let me lay my unused muzzle
across her lap, and let my claws
scratch lazily; and allow the water
to collect by the rocks, and slither
down the sunlit-chapeled face
of our rivulet; remember
I have never eaten quickened
warmth of bone and nerve and sinew
and the sweetest fleshy parts —
as I could take in blood-soft bites
the entire body of your daughter.

He decides to perambulate no farther
through *this* zoo; the wolf is howling
for the wayward offering.

The glass in front of the fence fills up
with a gaggle of strangers whose open mouths
mock him openly: "Why not throw her ...?"
And less literary elbows
point to him as to a fool.
He turns to wheel his lady outward,
who, in the studied loveliness
and stateliness of her generation,
drools and declines to notice this.

2. The Orangutan

it is as though a troll had wakened
to squeals and footfalls overhead
curved with its flat face the glass
of aqueous nightmares — the redheaded ape
meditates on the mouths of babes
they stare at one another with moony eyes
the babies try to pick their noses, too

3. The Hippos

hippos' heart-shaped assholes
sprout piggish tails
that brush away the flies and dirt
one can never tell
backwards where they've been
somnolent as clouds they move
across the cement compound
like cirrus on a hazy day
they don't seem to progress at all
yet always get someplace

4. The Jaguar

viaja solo y en la noche
the jaguar's errant eyes
mirror with unerring aim
the white protruding Adam's apple
pointed up at him

5. The Seals

the seals lurch in arcs around
and around the same old ground
held in water the way air
slips a pinion like a piston
ring around the sky

6. The Lemurs

the feral simian is overdone
God probably thought about making a rat
then changed his mind when he had the color —
dun-gray — of the fur and the Martian eyes
that widen with hates or loves or carnal
desires we know nothing of
they howl and chatter at everything
that is not part of them

7. The People

the schoolboy's been so educated
he calls the hippo elephant
and others with him think the fisher

marten is a fox
most have crocodiles on their shirts
and the Reptile House resounds
with roars and stinks and striking colors
green skins, pink tongues, and hidden fangs
and adolescent bellowings

8. The Lions

the lions lie bored beyond redemption
they agree with Forster that life is dull
exciting only by imagination
slightly perverse, slightly sexual
a lioness looks up from a stupor
gnawing with her eyes
calmly as one might look up on the plain
the unfinished ballet of a gazelle's
leg crunched in its mouth

9. The Spider Monkeys

the loop-tailed monkeys seem ambi-sexual
their curiosity about genitalia
explored and licked and poked and sucked
the ferrous-oxide eyes that catch
at shadows as at invisible vines
the yammering, the always busy
smelly coupling and bitchery
might evoke
the *Marquis de Sade's* disgust

10. *The Parrots*

if they could speak they would squawk as critics
in descending thirds of equivocation
they chew at cuds so contentedly
they should have been born as Brahman cows
don't tell me about the "bright flashing" colors
that are as remote as a mountain landscape
I don't like the looks of their necks when they turn
a yellow eye that squats in a skull
I don't care if they sing like tenors and sopranos
I wouldn't teach them to speak Esperanto

11. *The Black Leopard*

unto him all beauty draws
itself as to creation's source
the puling, squabbly faces below
might well exist on another planet
they look like nothing that he knows
he lies so still
lithe, lean and lustrous
the Saturn rings of his eyes
orbiting in order
only the tail
seems to flick a question
why such ugliness as ours
should stand on the other side of the bars

12. *Coda — Taking the Waters*

the four-faced clock tolls four
with a flourish of timpani
the leaves that are left, the mealy dust

that catches in your throat
all battened down by a misty rain
the tourists gone, the official shops
boarded up as for the winter
give the zoo the air of a seedy
German or Austrian resort
only the terminal ones left
behind without relatives or friends

Kirttimukha

I wake
to footfalls
of Steller's jays,
those clumsy-cone-headed aliens
that sound like turkey-gobblers
as they knock back pellets
of the cats' dry food.
Far out over the oat-grass hills,
in a shimmering track of mist
yellow fishing boats bob up like ducks
in a shooting gallery.

On the near hillside
calves bawl
for warm-wet teats.
The bored cows
extend their trumpet necks,
obbligato.
Among a meadow's night-born shoots
two trout-spotted fawns
twitch silky tails
and felt-tip noses.
A few feet away
the kitchen cats
stretch out at the foot of a cattail patch.
The light also rests there —
as if it had come home.

I think about existence in the city,
how what I see is tinged with dread,

as if I were witnessing a newspaper headline
in every approaching silhouette —
and all I hear's a boom-box tape
of sound-bite dislocations
or paranoid injustice-seekers
who plead with airplane-droning voices
the mathematical logic of their claims.

The footfall this time's the golden cat
plunking down at my crossed feet
a bowed-neck baby rabbit,
with its long back legs stuck out behind.
That's the Easter bunny, an ikon, I say,
clutched by blank-eyed, lead-limbed children
in shadow-tossing dreams.

Her second bite penetrates its anus
beneath its little cotton-tail —
the softest-pertest-private part.
I leave as she begins to masticate
and fill with blood her long-stiff whiskers.
As I slide the door
she looks up at me,
sunlight in her leaf-green eyes,
then belly-growls with satisfaction,
and begins to purr.
Sly puss, I say,
such a sly puss.

Taking a Bearing

A compass rose of ridges —
if rose could turn blue
the color of old ink
tracked across a letter,
with purple and indistinct
readings at the edges —
trembles all around me,
Blue Mountain to Canada.
A sweat-drying empty wind
(empty as an empty stomach)
shears across the tower
in the way that wind has
of mapping stony places —
of giving them all names
that sound just alike
but no one can pronounce.

Lord of no detail
but master of configuration
and the general idea —
at 48 I've managed
not to skip a beat
(or at least two or three)
or burst an artery
scraping the way up.
Although I might have trotted
to the top at twenty
without a hoarse breath
I like it better now
that sweaty satisfactions
dry out in the wind —

that there's no need to yodel
my arrival or my name.

Crouched, but unconcerned
by lightning and thunder,
I'm too tired perhaps to care
or even to wonder
how out of nowhere
storms magnify themselves
and build up from the back.
I like it better now
that my chest should burst
from pure overuse —
not suffocate from fancy
of an eye or face,
or suffer nightmare fears
of how the helpless die —
and that my heart's content
to do its work alone.

Wingin' On

Wingin' On, the name of a crossroads
in the prairie country of Oklahoma

Hawks made the only shadows
darkening the grass —
grass so dry it rattled
with every drift
of wind.

Wind was what I wanted —
a storm from the stars
that would uproot it all:
house, prairie, fields
of twenty-acre soy

beans that were so ugly
I should have burned them down.
I dreamed only of forces
so strong they could transform
my body into fire:

the house and all those in it
so scared they could not listen
to anything beyond
the roar of what I said.
I made myself a mate,

ethereal and thin —
not science but pure fiction.
I had her place the moon
in the place of dread
to shape his sleeping eyes

into starry visions —
a celestial
bestiary,
sweaty and mute,
dark with delight.

Speaking in Tongues

Yodeling, babbling, bug-eyed, shaking
Loose their hands from stiffened wrists,
They sought the spirit's higher tenor —
A cleaner, whiter corner of heaven —
An angel's wing on which to rest —

A song to take them from the body's
Aches and lusts, and old deceits —
A melody that Lucifer
Might take for pure light —
A clear way out of waywardness.

Drug from the back and made to kneel
And mumble to a Christ I thought who cared
No more for these sweaty lives than I ...
I heard my mother — to whom my soul
Was bonded faster than to any god —

Singing "Tenderly ... Jesus is coming ... "
I wanted to save her and myself —
To be taken up in the spirit's hymnal
Till we were of the purest gospel —
Till my rage was sweeter than a psalm.

As she lay still, of a broken back,
And tried to breathe through tubercular lungs
She might have called my name in the dark —
Though the preacher said the last thing she said
Was "Alle ... Alle ... Alleluia!"

Taken Away

"Don't whip that goddamned saw. Let
the tool do the work." The voice, low,
and guttural, and spent —
without emotion — meaning only what was meant.
This belted one stinks of gasoline.
I have been trimming the old maple all this
        morning,
and letting my thoughts idle like the saw
        in idle moments —
wasting the earth's bile, and raising my own.

"You son-of-a-bitch," I replied, to myself,
"Mother knows you raped my sister.
You're going to jail. You are going to
        jail!"
Yet his rhythm was like a rocking horse's —
steady as the hymn that feathered from his throat
        last Sunday morning
like some huge black bird with its yellow eyes
        blind on a paradise
of thirteen-year-old raven-haired maidens,
        like my sister.
Mother chimed, and took everything in.

In those woods I rocked from cloud to tree
and back to rock. From my pulpit-stump
I converted the heathen animals
(those he had not shot)
to a kind of pagan Christianity:
They were free to worship the old gods of crows,
        bluejays, sunlight,

meadows, clearings, the round of seasons,
        the clouds' tall ghost ships in procession —
only they must not *do* original sin.

They must not sin and yet be natural
as the gander and goose he bought my mother
for agreeing to come back to this "place
        forsaken"
(they collected us from the Children's Home
matrons bragged we might not leave).
The geese had never seen one another before
        but loved the other in watery reflections.
O it was a fairy beginning!
I thought all life must have the dignity,
        the slow devotions of those birds.

This rusty chair honks like a goose,
and I am reminded of their grave eyes
        and winding necks
as they saw my mother, taut as a hatchet.
She was killing all her garbled hopes and dreams —
        the shame of sickness, the shame of her children
in orphanages and foster homes.
She was deriding most the promises of men —
"the providers, the rapers of children."
If she could have managed it alone, she would that day
        have laid her own fevered neck across that bloody stump.

He arranged the yellow-eyed heads like question marks
back on their sockets,
and cupped the still-warm bodies side to side,
then held his own head in his hands,
as if he had been the one decapitated,
whiskery face blotched blue and red,

as an hour-glass flow of red dirt fluted
from the end of my shovel down to the white breasts.

"No need at all, no need at all." He strangled
and stuttered and started in with the saw,
and me, again — as if he found in that rhythm
    a poem or a prayer that said it all.
So we sweated on, working firewood for the night,
waiting for a siren to interrupt the drone
    and rasp of dialogue between us —
waiting till police forced us to abandon
    in mid-stroke steel teeth in bark
(the crosscut saw tilted toward the heavens)
and the guilt our bloody hands held in common.

Wanda Pickles

In the talent search you sang *Smoke Gets In Your Eyes*
In such a chanteuse way that Jack Pease and I
Stopped making fun of everything and
Goosing one another and the fat girls whose butts
Stuck out of those metal folding chairs
In the cafeteria-auditorium. Wanda Pikulski,
Touched by a magic wand — I mean smoke *did*
Get in our mean eyes and every boy in the 8th
And 9th grades dropped the drawers of adolescent
Adoration down to his ankles for the cross-eyed girl
Who never said more than an averted hi. Good-goddamn!
The sweet-strings-background music staticked out of
Those old bullhorn speakers, and above it and through it
And beyond it thrilled that unbelievable contralto voice,
Assured, controlled, husky in all the right places. And how
Dressed up you were in that low-cut gown, make-up, and no
Glasses, and the spotlight on you like a rouged Miss America.
When you repeated "When a lovely flame dies,"
A thousand 13-year-old hearts died right there with you and
    ached
For you never to stop. Wanda "Pickles," the nerdy duckling,
So sophisticated she could have been a movie star. And it
Wasn't just the song but the way you hung out over the edge
Of the melody, pushing it up and over the entire Lowell
Junior High Assembly, including the teachers in the back
Row — as if you were the heroine on a precipice
And kept hanging over, teetering there to our oohs and aahs
And the prayer of Sweet Jesus don't let her fall over. We knew
    in our
Nasty but innocent hearts that in a being so transformed
Into sweet celebrity, there was hope for us all.

That in the agony of acne and pimples that bled
And all those hormones ballooning in our bodies,
And voices that were adenoidal and sinus-hoarse —
That never repeated anything the way it was rehearsed
In the fever of imagination, where they were always suave
As Melvyn Douglas wooing society ladies
At the Orpheum Theater on Saturday night —
Where we never suffered the nerves of bad breath
Or had our voices, strangulated, break.
You were not only speaking but singing for us all,
And you brought the song off with a high crescendo
Leaving the last sibilant, the last liquid syllable
Like a soap bubble poised in the air,
Trembling with the promise of a rainbow life —
That if no one else loved us the god of awe did —
And in that stillness of opened mouths, that time to be moved
Like a light to the center of consciousness
Only a few times in our own dark lives,
Breathed a new gospel of art and song.

Sunday Morning – 1982

"Hi..." A cherub's honeyed voice lacquers
    the air.
She is holding a doll in her hands
and rocking from one foot to another
in front of a white frame house.
She calls me "Daddy" and there is so little
guile in eyes or limbs or grin
that I almost laugh in spite of myself
and the hangover mangling my head.
I want to rush over and pick her up
and hold her doll's cheek against my own.
I want to look straight at her blue
and dark-lashed eyes, and her baby-white teeth,
and say that I'll always let her live
in the cave of my arms — that in spite
of the sourness of my tongue
and belly, and surly spirit, I'll sing
the soul of this child in circles to heaven.
But of course I dare not ...
so I walk on
with an odd, perfunctory salute.

Over the second beer I begin to wonder:
little girls have always loved me,
I say to myself, because I was a brother
with five younger sisters. I expected their allegiance,
and was fierce and protective. That is why children,
strange and kin, are not afraid of me now,
but take my hand as if I were a brother,
and we could walk on forever.

This reverie, boozy and sentimental,
and the Sunday Times (the Yankees won
and so did the Mets) have lulled me so
I hardly notice the photograph
of a child in Lebanon, a little girl
with stubby hands and grimy eyes.
Tears have dug furrows into her cheeks,
and she looks as lost as the rubble around her.
A Homeless Child, the caption reads.
She will starve or be killed herself or raped
    or hardened
into the likeness of a murderer.
As I read the story
it is like stepping through
the defecations
of politicians.

And I remember the stories from Guatemala
and El Salvador of bayoneted
pregnant women, and children's severed
heads and limbs, of bodies beaten sodden
and tossed like scrap on a pile of already
rotting corpses. I remember the photographs
    of Jews
from World War II concentration camps
and how we kids all turned our heads
when the ovens were first shown on newsreel films
between Gene Autry and Roy Rogers. I remember
the sparkle, like dew on the grass, at dawn
when the sun promises nothing but long, slow heat
and cicadas lazing in trees; afternoons
when the light in an eye and the curve
    of a hip
were an invitation to be part of the grass.

Hitchhikers, 1936, Walker Evans

She seems to be seeing something special,
something in particular
that shies away from the camera;
and he could be directing
Model A's down the gravel highway
idly with his thumb.

Even though the photograph is gray,
I know the color of their eyes
is midnight-blue, and I know those eyes
mirror Gable and Colbert —
that their two hearts, desperate as one,
filled with animated light,

know that what happened in "It Happened One Night"
will happen to them, if only they wait —
if only they keep walking backwards,
if only they ignore
the grating, straight-ahead concerns
leaving them behind.

Dull Knife in Nebraska

Strong with sweat, tobacco,
cold wind flavored with a thousand miles
of rubble and the rubble of reservations
disheveled in his clothes —
straight down from the Dakotas
he makes a stand in the doorway
of this rest stop for the bleary.
Weighing one foot and then the other,
as though the waltz of freight trains
          rocked his gait,
eyes like jugs of Thunderbird,
he mixes the acid of apprehension
and fear of feral things
in all the well-stocked guts
of the soft, white creatures
crawled from cars
with their own mouth-tightened spite.

The Poet François de Montcorbier (des Loges) Resurrects a Soul in Grand Central Station

in her violet bath
sunk in *La Belle Époque*
maids speak in *voix céleste*
and call her *mademoiselle*
one sprinkles stars of soap the other
bends with a robe
so exquisite with *voile*
butterflies might migrate there
instead of to Mexico

the colony of hairs above her lip
lisp like those on a milch cow's udder
they too catch the froth
from the teats of milk and honey
paranoia with its foam
bleeds through the peeling lustre
of the eyes' onion light
her speech scrapes like the mother
of old sailors on a rocky beach

perhaps the "dice of drowned men's bones"
(green eyes of a drowning poet)
"toss" in the rattles of her cup
asshole, lips, puckered vagina
bind her to a *Trinity*
so pissed and puked and creased
she could be the *Maria* whose prayer I ghosted
in our religious century
a pox on those who out of habit
    live and fear to die

Rockville Court

*Even the happy mortals we term ordinary
or commonplace act out their own mental
tragedies and live a far deeper and wider
life than we are inclined to believe pos-
sible in the light of our prejudices....*
— *Edwin Arlington Robinson*

Whether they were crazed
By drugs or religion —
The Jesus Freaks whose story
Ran last week in the paper —
The husband bolted cyanide,
The wife had a secret smile.
The lawyers and the judge
Must have seemed so stupid
To her as she sat down
(She had just caressed his head
Before it went bumping
With the rest of him
Along the polished floor),
Carefully placed the pill
On the tip of her tongue and swallowed:
For better or for worse
Tracey followed William.

Judge Frosh was so amazed
By the noise made
From hands, feet, and heads
Threshing on the floor,
And the hoarse death screams
(The last contribution
Made to this life
By Melton and his wife)
He desisted from intoning
"Controlled environments."
His face went out of order.

I think of famous lovers:
Tristan and Iseult,
Their "uncreated light";
Of Romeo and Juliet
In Shakespeare's intellect,
How he manipulated
Them into a moral:
Why it seems so right
That innocents must die.
Order in disorder.

(The best was Villon
For his paraphrase,
"*Pour ung plaisir mille doulours,*"
And his good advice,
"*Bien est eureux qui riens n'y a.*")

I think of Robinson's others —
Happy, commonplace,
Who act out tragedies
Over breakfast news —

The younger wife who reads
With horrified content
Of those who writhed to death
In a Rockville court.

I feel her mouth go slack
While her mind's enchanted
By something absolute.

Note: Galway Kinnell's translation of
Villon's 15th-century idiomatic French:
   "For every joy a thousand sorrows;
   Better the man who has no part in it."

Quartered With the Sun

1.

say a thousand
maybe more
thin flat wrists
of poplars
broke over the edge of a sea-flat prairie
never quite reaching out enough
to touch one another's
trembling hands
but shaking with the effort

2.

trees so full of windy discourse
yesterday stand mute
dark as dream-configurations
speechless at dawn
as if the Spanish moss of rain
curling through this early morning
issued from the heart of night
(like a paranoid's homeless scream
on Mulberry Street at 5 a.m.

3.

please I need my parents
someone take care of me
steam rises from my coffee

Rome still reverberates
from Old St. Patrick's campanile
pigeons also coo and strut
and send soft patters down the walls
where photographers from *Vogue* and *Elle*
on Paris-bookstall afternoons

contort in front of crewcut models
costume-balled in scarecrow-black)
now on Lake Forest's criss-crossed path
a coffee mug tilts cold and stagnant
gypsy-red
among the algae-faced reflections
I jig with it clapped upon my head
dancing-warm in the natural litter
a monkey chained to the windy gods
        quartered with the sun

Digital Analysis

The pathologist shows us pain
on the backs of hands, on the
delicate windowshades of eyes —
the way those coordinates of veins

knot, herniate. This patient,
78 today, died
yesterday. Look at his life,
the small map of it

traced blue on a bulging lid —
and there beneath a rib
the pulse of all he loved
rose on famished blood

to fight for its share
of blood with common air.
An absence of raw upheavals
smooths these sheeted forms —

as though they had succumbed
to angelic entreaty —
as though they had learned too much
at the last moment and must be still:

each filed away, with its name
and vital information
intoned by an orderly
with breathless persiflage

as he finishes hog-tying
a tag to the last big toe,
then rolls the drawer back
with a flourish, with a snap.

The Midnight Wrestling Show

The roses in his cheeks shadow night
The way a train shadows its track
Down a long grade, the headlight limning
A bestiary of blood.
We all know murder
Reflected in its fact
Is nothing but fiction
Left to its own infractions.
But I am talking about the wrestler,
The feisty clown acting as an actor,
Shadow of sweat and subterfuge.

We shall not gall him loser or winner.
He is the rose in the rose-colored glass
("Thou art indeed just, Lord, if I contend
With thee; but, sir,
So what I plead is just").
When he looks in the mirror after
The latest one-night stand
He tells little stories —
Like the ones we tell ourselves in the morning.
The washrag he holds to his head
Reddens with the common salt.

Bloodsong

The rain's original voice
is barely orphic now.
What is heard is old —
the ear a chipped shell —
as though the surf of history
left but wrack.

If only I could know the rain —
if only the rain were fastened
to anything
more skeleton than sky.

But rain accompanies itself.
Those who lie alone at night,
those whose dream-sweats bead their mouths
with hopes beyond the ordinary
rise through waves of sleep to listen
for the rain to make more sense than sound.

Bloodsong's low as evening rain.
It is the breath all sleepers take.
It rises with the dawn wind
in open places,
and falls with the shadows
in empty rooms —
shadows morning moves
from one place to another.

Eudaemonia

That leaf, a crop
drone-ants work,
antennae dosed with the power of purpose.
They know exactly what they want
from syrupy chlorophyll.
They know to a T the lines they march
from one predetermined point to another,
regular as stars.

If I were to crush the leaf I examine,
if I were to cause loss of consciousness
and yawing vertigo —
if I pinched its rhubarb-colored stem
and balled the sticky leaf in my hands
to scraps and twisted small brown bodies —
if I built a blaze of epidermis
and immolated these Moloch-minded
minions of "unalterable law" —
my palms would feel a numb elation,
my mind a secret satisfaction.

Speech After Long Silence

feverish and mumbling
disheveled in a lawn chair
thighs too heavy
to hold together
she doesn't care
about the whistling
neighbor rubbing down his car
she doesn't care that he worships tin
and trim and flowers that grow just so

she doesn't want to be helped to the house
and folded into bed
to have to look up at eyes
bored with the bad joke
of her ineptitude
day after dull day
she wants to go on laughing
and whispering to herself
what nobody knows

she wants to go on tying
the knots of her hands
into pretty patterns
she wants her death
make-believe
the white pallet the moon
spreads across the leaves
is like a fairytale
turning dark at the edges

she wants to be
both guest and body
at her funeral
away from visiting relatives
with ceaseless children
who run about
with large blank eyes
and one-line mouths
honking loud as geese

she wants to go back to the mountains
so high in silent country
her breathing will be loud
she wants to be like clouds
parted by the moon
she wants to navigate the sky
through the length of one long night
lie on the meadows
like mist through a country dawn

Note: *The title is from the first line of a poem by Yeats,*
After Long Silence.

Waking Up in Rabun Gap, 1988

In Memoriam,
Edie Christy, 1939-1988,
dear companion

say bird at the window pane
deftly refereeing
an amateur tennis match
of serve-and-volley moths
eyes wide from ululations
that woke a slumped body
like a natural alarm
say five o'clock in the morning
the forgotten lamp's
pilgrim light
prostrate on a mosque of carpet
say bits of powdered wings
stuck to a window screen
like one of those Schnabel paintings
stuck up from remains
of the 1980's last supper
say tall morning woods
rusting in first light
the sun torqued in a creek
acetylene tongue
welding Edie's waterfall
(her grace and heart's amplitude
jailed in the cracked red dirt)
say jewels of the grass
on a mountain meadow
flash their fragmentary lives

Rattlesnake Cove

The plumed tails of fleeing horses,
sun dappled through their porcelain hooves,
make flywheels of dusty light and motion.

When their sonic booms rebound
on our waxed tympanic membrane
close-up in a field there is no room

for anything
but thickening
wisps from sweaty fear.

Stuck to ourselves, sundial shadows
threaded on unlimbering grass,
we start at the crunch of a foot on gravel.

Our host assures us the name's a misnomer,
no snakes in this part of California
since the first Franciscans — the horses, yearlings,

conjure in their ghost-eyes Quetzalcoatl
rattling where ledges lean only on shadows.
Human history, archetypal,

made Biblical heroes petty and vindictive,
while Indians leaned toward the heavens,
connecting stars to story-telling gods.

The word, corporeal,
the word for snake, cloud-rattling-shadow —
fear is nameless but it tastes familiar,
        alkaline, the first breath of morning.

We quote computer, silicon technology,
the inchoate twenty-first century —
a century our children covet —

and debate whether serpent superstitions
will shadow their lives — the way that cloud,
        that pentagonal beast's
greyhounds harry sinewy plumage

in flight on flintrock promontories —
while we exclaim extravagantly
the ancient directions the blood still takes.

Surfcasting at Montauk Point

the earth's sideways movement
through the stars

the wind's huge jet engines
shut down

at 4 a.m.
I, vaudevillian

bounce and rattle
through the dark

the flashlight in the basket
of this old rusty bike

my own small antenna
poking through the static

in the awry undergrowth
tricks? I'm 51

and pedal standing up
Montauk Indians

clap with one hand
I hesitate through history

above an ocean rumble
balancing a fishing stick

across a wire that zings
100 million murdered voices

(humans tortured, blood-mouth dead
in this our 20th century)

from earth to the sidereal regions
sotto voce Agnus Dei

the sea booms its chorus
in swells of tall-green-seaweed faces

crickets, ghosts, take your pick
in mezzanine and orchestra

roll up the starry curtain
I am keeping it simple now

I am letting the silent flesh sing
in the phosphorescent dark

Snow Woman

While I was an orphan
I made up a mother
entirely of snow

I erected her
transient head and body
deep in woods that flanked

the fields we sweated summers
I filled her with the light
that exposed trees

on dark and muffled days
when it lit up clouds
and flashed our photograph

classic son and mother
her arm on my shoulder
in our element

sometimes when I stopped
angling the arm
and brushing new snow

from her *kouroi* eyes
I heard a breath's intake
my own in alarm

that a matron might have followed
with unbelieving ears
our gossipy conversation

or all the other orphans
had discovered my adoption
and cawed like crows

though we hardly talked aloud
she always spoke her mind
with lovely inclinations

of course I was a changeling
under the spell of Circe
who cursed my father Odysseus

I keened with her through March
I pounded all her parts
till my hands turned brutal

I prayed to the skies
for a long ghost ship of snow
turning sideways with the wind

but her posture slumped
the almond-shaped eyes
and Grecian features blurred

the ones I closely modeled
on a photograph
torn from that old book

I sang her death song
through sunlight and shadow
to the stars' benisons

I held the wasted form
till in her crumbling breasts
blood mixed with water

Untitled

I want the stillness of snow in woods
when big-slow pieces trail down through trees
and the lights have gone out in all the houses
and snow is alone with itself — alone
with that other hush
that only the sick and wounded hear.
I want to close my eyes and imagine snow
drifting down on them —
as if I were a fallen tree lying out in a field,
as if I didn't care any more about the living,
the always-trying of one breath on another,
but settled myself in to breathe like snow
and the planet's slow turning through the starry dark.
I don't want to think of anything ahead
but more and more infinite and infinite spaces
and more and more stillness, more and more dark.
I want to remember when I was falling and dying
late last summer, the ambulance and helicopter,
and how I lay there like a weathered log
being pushed and prodded
busily back toward a loud life.
I want to remember how I turned away —
how I wished they would all just leave me alone —
for I was imagining winter then,
seeing range after range of mountain woods
lit up by dark lamps of snow.
As I sank in cold-sweat lakes of pain,
as I passed out again and again,
I came to enjoy such a sweet relief
I was like a child, the only one awake
in a houseful of strangers,

the one who goes to a balcony
and puts his hands on the snowy railing
and feels his body draw back from the cold
but is so enchanted by the spectacle of snow
in darkness and stillness
he decides to walk out in the woods and sleep there.
And so amid the sharp-cold voices,
    the needles and tubes and lights,
my body swollen and feverish,
I was walking through woods
in the fiery dark,
I was a candle burning,
I was a light in the distance,
I was wind where the wind dies down with a hush,
I was a slender tree,
I was someone who keeps on going the wrong way,
I was one of those small animals
    whose homes are never found,
I was a child trailing through snow
back to its own world.

Revenants

I

The amber-eyed foxes bit your shoulder
was what we thought when we spied you
calculating us in the shower.
After the slightest-momentary moment
of blank-eyed reverie you turned
in panic to a role-model from the movies:
a dowager's imperceptible nod
tossed a bouquet of perfume in the air like violets.
Our doltish mouths
opened and closed like horses' nostrils.
We shied away from the afterglow
of shrewd-bright eyes, the flash of blood
high on those bladed cheeks —
turning brighter than bordello lamps.
We were cavalry officers booted round a table
in a briefing room. We wore high tunics
and riding breeches. We came to the point
with guttural German expletives
and swagger sticks. Naked under that table
you groveled from one set of knees to another
and the empurpled staffs aloft the stiff twill.

II

We regarded you as the long-lost mother,
rich and matronly but sexy too,
with toilet-watered bosom, and under-things
so light and filmy they must take minutes
to reach the bedroom floor.
Ooh-la-la! Eleven-year-old boys,
our fantasies swooned to incoherence,
our attitudes into stereotypes — frog-eyed guffaws
and vomity grins — our faces red
not only from sexual stimulation but shame
too gurgled in our bowels — we felt as Susannah
watched by the elders.
There in the Tulsa Children's Home
the simile of boys with prisoner-fathers
was a poetry workshop taught at night by matrons —
leathery-old-loutish women
who branded with switches and razor-strops
birth-mark-bright limbs in that same shower.

III

Fur stoles with heads went almost out of fashion
before I found you in New York
slumming at the old-style White Horse Tavern
among the bohemians of '58.
I was of course young and certain women adored me —
the kind who write to prisoners,
the kind who prefer their violence straight,
low-class and slanderous — the type
whose fathers beat them for their own good.
Surrounded by those poets of the moment
who milled around your exotic furs
and Miss Porter's accent, on exhibit,
you turned on me as if surprised.
I thought your eyes like reveries,
and the small brush fires that flickered in your voice
demanded boots to stamp them out.
My unconscious mind sang like a chorus
of pre-pubescent boys.

IV

I made you pay for everything.
I gouged you for clothes, the apartment rent,
champagne and oysters. In the restaurants
you showed me the moves with a knife and fork
European-style. You straightened out my drawl
into mock-Southern-Ivy-League. In the good museums
you talked about how the eye is drawn in
to walk a work's interiors.
I thrilled at singers and pliéd with the corps.
Your tastes were high and infallible
except when it came to men.
I made you walk *my* interiors —
homemade landscapes by Edvard Munch.
I nagged about your advantages
even in bed when the strings of sex
were still but resonant.
I shouted out injustices
with details graphed from the Children's Home,
the State Orphanage, the reform-school years —
I taunted you from your own mink coat.
I exulted in your crying — the tears
left salty residue.

V

We dithered around
the depths of sado-masochistic sex,
a little paddling, a little rough handling.
I made believe I was a stevedore
with loud tattoos
who held you up
then held you down.
The childhood you would have made a donation
like a blood transfusion, arm to arm,
I strained around your bent swan neck.
Thirsting with idealistic guilt
you swallowed it all — until one night, drunk,
I snarled the story of Lady Bountiful
who had blundered on boys in a communal shower —
of the other ladies from the Junior League,
bored, fur-coated, and perfumed,
who escorted us to movies once a year,
who sat through howlers by Laurel and Hardy
and never opened their glamourous mouths.

VI

I loved the ironic idea of you
as a kind of emotional Bombay beggar.
I coveted abstractions and absences —
no leftover breath, no familiar toilette,
no warm but soiled body
to mold myself in the morning to.
I killed while love was still dramatic,
innocent of banality.
Excluding you was an aesthetic act.

Your ordinary weathers I would never know.
How you might sit by a kitchen window
in an old robe while the light advances
square by square across the tiled floor
and the morning thoughts come and collect you
and take you here and there.
Back even to an ersatz poet in The Village
30 years ago, whose name you do not recall
immediately, and whose face
is a birthmark blur of intensity.

The tea you make this time has leaves
that plaster themselves against the sides
of the empty cup. The more you stare
at them the more they look like bodies,
fallen, pointed, perpendicular,
Hieronymous Bosch might have arranged.

Verdigris

for Nina, Hanukkah-Christmas, 1989

Swiss powdered soup, Italian water
cold from a courtyard spigot,
splashed into a Boy Scout camp-cook pot,
a tea bag of Tuscan herbs
lowered into this verdigris ...
flames from a Sterno can
scorching the slick aluminum,
dyeing a ring on the Florentine floor —
tiles so bleached the pairs of long-robed figures
linked across them look like stains.
You, kneeling, brushing hair
back with one hand while the other
trails a spoon that steers the crusts
and bubbles breaking on the soup.

We knew the dog of the concierge
across the street only by its yowling
that went off, wolf-like, with the Catholic bells
on Sunday mornings. Their resonance
and the lone coyote-calling,
half-clown and half-saint,
disturbed us like half-waking dreams.
We dubbed him "born again,"
the saint of Sunday mornings,
the wolf that nips the stolid sheep
and herds them out to Elysian pastures

where God like Moses with flint-rock eyes
pinches the Devil with a witching wand
that makes him spring up straight
and speak in tongues.

We liked our mornings still
on the stone courtyard stairs
cool with condensation,
heavy with trellises
of dewy morning glories,
our milk and coffee aerial,
the wall shadows evaporating.

Firenze, 1966, Prince Street, 1989 —
I think as I watch the blue gas flames
raise the kettle to a soprano pitch
of that albergo and its name —
"Speranza e Commercio" —
how it was so unthinkable then
to link commerce with hope,
or predict I would move those shadowed mornings
back toward today.
I see your kneeling figure where
you were only 19, the grave-blank face,
a girl's graveness,
a figure I might have seen in Hals,
a late teen-age girl and her grieving —
the loneliness of unbound breasts
tendered to a room of drunken men.

When I bring our coffee to the bed
the spiderwebs on your sleeping face,
the inaudible breath, the tide of dreaming
trembling through a fisted hand,
break in my throat a tuneless song,
and I want to howl like that dumb dog

for the nameless feelings that will not be stilled,
for the charity of women's bodies —
for the veins that climb your thighs
like blue morning glories.